First World War
and Army of Occupation
War Diary
France, Belgium and Germany

59 DIVISION
176 Infantry Brigade
Prince of Wales's (North Staffordshire Regiment)
1/5 Battalion.
1 February 1918 - 31 May 1918

WO95/3021/1

The Naval & Military Press Ltd
www.nmarchive.com
Published in association with The National Archives

Published by

The Naval & Military Press Ltd

Unit 10 Ridgewood Industrial Park,

Uckfield, East Sussex,

TN22 5QE England

Tel: +44 (0) 1825 749494

www.naval-military-press.com

www.nmarchive.com

This diary has been reprinted in facsimile from the original. Any imperfections are inevitably reproduced and the quality may fall short of modern type and cartographic standards.

© Crown Copyright
Images reproduced by permission of The National Archives, London, England, 2015.

Contents

Document type	Place/Title	Date From	Date To
Heading	WO95/3021/1		
Heading	59 Div 176 Bde 5 Bn North Staffs Regt 1918 Feb-1918 May		
Heading	War Diary of 5th Bn North Staffs Regiment From 1st Feby 1918 To 28th Feby 1918 Vol 13		
War Diary	Liencourt	01/02/1918	08/02/1918
War Diary	Bienvillers	09/02/1918	09/02/1918
War Diary	Ervillers (belfast Camp)	10/02/1918	12/02/1918
War Diary	Mory (South Camp)	13/02/1918	16/02/1918
War Diary	Noreuil Sector	17/02/1918	28/02/1918
Miscellaneous	Attached Appendies for the 14th February 1918	14/02/1918	14/02/1918
Heading	59th Division 176th Infantry Brigade War Diary 5th Battalion North Staffordshire Regiment March 1918		
Heading	War Diary of 5th Bn North Staffs Regiment From 1st March 1918 To 31st March 1918 Vol 14		
War Diary	Noreuil Sector	01/03/1918	10/03/1918
War Diary	Mory (Nr Camp)	11/03/1918	19/03/1918
War Diary	Bullecourt (Sector)	20/03/1918	21/03/1918
War Diary	Douchy-Les-Ayette	22/03/1918	23/03/1918
War Diary	Bouzincourt	24/03/1918	25/03/1918
War Diary	Beaucourt	26/03/1918	26/03/1918
War Diary	Candas	27/03/1918	28/03/1918
War Diary	Caucourt	29/03/1918	31/03/1918
Heading	176th Brigade 59th Division 1/5th Battalion North Staffordshire Regiment April 1918		
Heading	War Diary of 5th Bn North Staffs Regiment From 1st April 1918 To 30th April 1918 Vol 15		
War Diary	Caucourt	01/04/1918	01/04/1918
War Diary	Watou Area	02/04/1918	10/04/1918
War Diary	Ypres	11/04/1918	11/04/1918
War Diary	Passchendaele	12/04/1918	12/04/1918
War Diary	Vlamertinghe	13/04/1918	13/04/1918
War Diary	Reninghelst	13/04/1918	13/04/1918
War Diary	Locre	13/04/1918	14/04/1918
War Diary	Bailleul	14/04/1918	18/04/1918
War Diary	Boeschepe	19/04/1918	20/04/1918
War Diary	Peselhoek	20/04/1918	21/04/1918
War Diary	Oost Cappel	22/04/1918	26/04/1918
War Diary	Poperinghe	27/04/1918	27/04/1918
War Diary	Ouderdom	28/04/1918	30/04/1918
Heading	War Diary of 5th North Staffs Regiment From 1st May 1918 To 31st May 1918 Vol 16		
War Diary	Ouderdom	01/05/1918	05/05/1918
War Diary	Watou	06/05/1918	06/05/1918
War Diary	St Momelin Area	07/05/1918	10/05/1918
War Diary	Mametz	11/05/1918	11/05/1918
War Diary	Nedonchelle	12/05/1918	14/05/1918
War Diary	Magnicourt	15/05/1918	15/05/1918
War Diary	Hautville	16/05/1918	20/05/1918
War Diary	Magnicourt	21/05/1918	21/05/1918

War Diary	Livossart	22/05/1918	24/05/1918
War Diary	Mametz	25/05/1918	29/05/1918
War Diary	Clarques	30/05/1918	31/05/1918
Operation(al) Order(s)	5th Bn. North Stafford Regiment Operation Order No. 5	08/05/1918	08/05/1918
Operation(al) Order(s)	Operation Order No.1 By Lieut-Col. T.H.S. Swanton, Commanding 5th North Staffs Regt. Bn. Training Staff.	09/05/1918	09/05/1918
Operation(al) Order(s)	Operation Order No 2 by Lt Col J.H.S. Swanton Commanding 5th North Staff Regt Bn Training Staff	10/05/1918	10/05/1918
Operation(al) Order(s)	Operation Order No. 5 By Lieut-Col. T.H.S. Swanton Commanding Centre Group	19/05/1918	19/05/1918

690 302

59 DIV
176 BDE

5 BN. NORTH. STAFFS REGT

1918 FEB — 1918 MAY.

(absorbed 2/5 BN JAN 1918)

FROM 46 DIV 137 BDE
TO 39 DIV — 116 BDE

2/5" Bn N. STAFF REG

1918

3021

Army Form C. 2118.

WAR DIARY
~~INTELLIGENCE SUMMARY.~~
(Erase heading not required.)

WS/13

Confidential

Original War Diary
of
5th Bn. North Staffs. Regiment

From:- 1st Feby 1918
To:- 28th Feby 1918

Army Form C. 2118.

WAR DIARY
or
INTELLIGENCE SUMMARY
(Erase heading not required.)

Volume No 2.
Page 66

5th Bn North Staffs. Regt. T.F.

February 1918

Instructions regarding War Diaries and Intelligence Summaries are contained in F.S. Regs., Part II. and the Staff Manual respectively. Title Pages will be prepared in manuscript.

Place	Date	Hour	Summary of Events and Information	Remarks and references to Appendices
LIENCOURT	1.		In G.H.Q Reserve (VI Corps Third Army) Company & Individual Training	Maps LENS II A/m 1/100,000
"	2.		Batt. Drill & Compound Training. The undermentioned officers posted to this unit from the Ups. North Staffs Regt. are posted to the Companies as under:— Capt. F.E. Wenger M.C. posted to "A" Coy. Lt. L.C. Comiskaw M.C. " " D " 2/Lt. L.C. Grice " " D " 2/Lt. G.M. Humphry " " B " Capt. N. Settle " " C "	A/m
"	3.			
"	4.		Church Parade. Brigade Route March. Route - Crossroads, LIENCOURT - I.25.3.5.3. - DENIER - LIGNEREUIL. I.12.a.3.3. - I.12.d.5.9 - BEAUFORT - LIENCOURT	A/m Cell.
"	5.		The 196th Infantry Brigade is inspected by the Corps Commander A/m. In the afternoon football match played by the 5th Batt Royal Staffs Regt. N.7. Company & Platoon Training. Final Assaulton Range.	A/m
"	6.		Battn. Drill	A/m
"	7.		Honours & Awards.	
"	8.		L/Sgt P. Rowley awarded the Belgian Croix de Guerre. The 196th Infantry Brigade is moved by Route March to the BIENVILLERS area. The 5th Batt. North Staffs Regt. moved to BIENVILLERS via LIENCOURT - Crossroads 0.10 C.5.59 SOMBRIN - SAULTY - 16m. via ARRAS-DOULLENS road 0.10 C.5.59 thence east along main Road to Y5 2.2.2 - LA-CAUCHIE - POMMIERS to BIENVILLERS.	A/m 51 CI. LENS II 1/40,000 1/100,000 A/m
BIENVILLERS	9.		In Corps Reserve. The Batt. is moved by Route March to BIENVILLERS - BUCQUOY NE via ABLAINZEVILLE - COURCELLES - CONTÉ-ERVILLERS - HANNESCAMPS. The 56th Division facing from GHQ Reserve to Corps Reserve at 12 Noon	A/m

2449 Wt. W14957/M90 750,000 1/16 J.B.C. & A. Forms/C.2118/12.

Army Form C. 2118.

WAR DIARY or INTELLIGENCE SUMMARY

(Erase heading not required.)

VOLUME No 2.
Instructions regarding War Diaries and Intelligence Summaries are contained in F. S. Regs., Part II. and the Staff Manual respectively. Title Pages will be prepared in manuscript.

Page 64

5th Batt. North Staffs Regt. T.F.

February 1918.

Place	Date	Hour	Summary of Events and Information	Remarks and references to Appendices
ERVILLERS (Belfast Camp)	10.		In Corps Reserve. Company & Platoon training	SICK LENS 11 Offr 4,000 / 100,000
"	11.		" "	Offr /
"	12.		The Battalion is moved by route march to MORY. South Camp & passes into Divisional Reserve.	
MORY (South Camp)	13.		In Divisional Reserve.	On
"	14.		The Battalion employed in providing working parties first ordered, are replaced that the 5th N. Staffs will relieve the 2/6 N. Staffs on the line on the night of 16/17th Feb. Bathing Parade	On
"			The Battalion receives the following award for most conspicuous bravery & initiative during the recent operations on the CAMBRAI Offensive:— L/Cpl John Thomas C. Company. The Victoria Cross. General Salutation of 6 working parties.	See letter attached
"	15.		The Battalion is moved by Route March to NOREUIL for the purpose of relieving the 2/6 N. Staffs Regt in the right Brigade Sub Sector.	Maps 51.b1.57C 1/20,000
"	16.		The relief being reported complete about 9 p.m.	On
NOREUIL SECTOR.	17.		The Battalion holding the line in the right Brigade Sub Sector, Army front. Coborate of Series of advanced posts, other Companies in the front. one in support & one in reserve. The dispositions of the Bn. are as follows:— C. Company holding a line from C11. a. 13.90 to GOOLE E. ALLEY (inclusive) with Class Platoons on the front line, one Platoon in HALIFAX SUPPORT. at 1 m. IKLEY SUPPORT with Coy. HQ at C5.d.6.65. B Company holding line extending from GOOLE ALLEY to U.29. c. 85.58 (Rt inclusive) 2 Platoons in front line at U.29 d 6g 23. D Coy in support in HORSE SHOE SUPPORT Coy HQ at U.29 d 11.29. 2 Plats in support, 2 Plats in DEWSBURY TRENCH. HQ at RAILWAY RESERVE & 2 Plats in NOREUIL-ECOUST Rd North C11. a 3.0. A Coy in reserve in the NOREUIL-ECOUST Rd north Coy HQ at C9.d.88.56. Battalion H.Q. at C11.c.70.95 "R.A.P.	On

Army Form C. 2118.

WAR DIARY
or
INTELLIGENCE SUMMARY
(Erase heading not required.)

VOLUME 2
Page 68

Instructions regarding War Diaries and Intelligence Summaries are contained in F.S. Regs., Part II. and the Staff Manual respectively. Title Pages will be prepared in manuscript.

5th Batt. North Staff's Regt.

February 1918

Place	Date	Hour	Summary of Events and Information	Remarks and references to Appendices
NOREUIL SECTOR	18.		The Battalion relieving the line on the right Brigade sub-sector.	The Batt S.P. S.W.4 NW.2
"	19.		The Battalion relieving the line on the right Brigade sub-sector engaged on wiring & carrying parties	1000 Other ranks
"	20.		"	Other
"	21.		"	
"	22.		Commencing at dusk "A" & "B" (company) relief took place. "D" Coy relieving "C" Coy on the right front. "B" Coy (one platoon) of "A" Coy returning "B" Coy at left front. "B" Coy (one platoon) of "A" Coy moved to Ilkley taking the place of "B" Coy (one platoon) moved to the reserves as follows "B" Coy at C5.d 1 to 5. Also W29.i.60.33. Coy distribution as follows "B" Coy at "A" Coy at C5.b (relief reported complete at 7.30 pm B Coy C11.a.3.0 & B Coy at C9.d.88.56.	Other
"	23.		The Battalion holding the line on the right Brigade sub-sector	Other
"	24.		"	Other
"	25.		"	Other
"	26.		The Battalion was organised as shown the night the following postures taken up A"B" Coy holding a line from C11.3.1 to C5.d trench 2 platoons in the front line, 1 platoon in support 1 platoon in Halifax Trench C11.b.3.1. "D" Coy 2 plats in front line with 2 plats in support at Coode Alley & Ilkley Support 1 plat in Horse Shoe Support. Coy HQ at C5.d.9.6.5. "A" Coy 3 plats holding a line from W29.d.35.75 to W29.c.9.6. 1 platoon in Apex dugout with "B" Coy HQ remaining at C9.d.88.56 C.H.H.Q at W29.5.60.26. Rotherham Alley & New Trench only held by the 2 Coys on the two Coys opened the Reserve Battalion moving forward. B.H Q'd R.A.P. at Sunken Road at C11.c.70.95	Other

2449 Wt. W14957/M90 750,000 1/16 J.B.C. & A. Forms/C.2113/12.

Army Form C. 2118.

WAR DIARY
or
INTELLIGENCE SUMMARY

(Erase heading not required.)

5th Batt. North Staffs Regt. T.F.

February 1918

Place	Date	Hour	Summary of Events and Information	Remarks and references to Appendices
NOREUIL Sector	27.		The Battalion Relieving the line in the Right Brigade Sub-Sector.	57B SW4. 57C NW3. 57C SW 1/10,000 57C 1/40,000
"	28.		Commencing at dusk the Battalion was relieved by the 2/6 North Staff Regt. On completion of relief the following disposition were occupied:	
			B Coy in DEWSBURY TRENCH "A" Coy in PONTEFRACT TRENCH	
			C Coy " ICAREE CORNER "D" TRENCH of INTERMEDIATE LINE	Qu
			B.H.Q. in NOREUIL-LONGATTE Rd at Q.d 8656	
			C.10 a & c. B.10 c & d. 8.	
			RAP at C.10.c.7.8. The relief being reported complete about 11 pm when the Battalion became the Reserve Battalion.	

Henry Johnson
Lt. Col.
Commanding 5th North Staffs Regt.

Attack of Appleghee
for the 14th February 1918.
Demicourt House & Cemicourt

L/Cpl. John Thomas is awarded
the VICTORIA CROSS for most
conspicuous bravery & initiative in
action. He saw the enemy making
preparations for a counter attack, &
with a comrade on his own initiative
decided to make a close reconnaissance.
These two went out in broad daylight
in full view of the enemy & under
heavy machine gun fire. His comrade
was hit within a few yards of the
trench, but undeterred L/Cpl Thomas
went on alone. Working round a
small copse he shot three snipers &
then pushed on to a building used by
the enemy as a night post. From
here he saw whence the enemy were
bringing up their troops & where they
were congregating. He stayed in
this position for an hour, sniping the
enemy the whole time & doing great
execution. He returned to our lines,
after being away three hours, with
information of the utmost value,

which enabled definite plans to be made and artillery fire to be brought on the line of formation so that when the attack took place it was broken up.

59th Division.
176th Infantry Brigade.

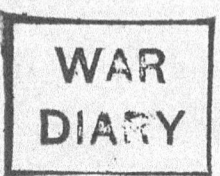

5th BATTALION

NORTH STAFFORDSHIRE REGIMENT

MARCH 1 9 1 8

Army Form C. 2118.

WAR DIARY
or
INTELLIGENCE SUMMARY.

(Erase heading not required.)

Original War Diary
of
5th Bn North Staffs Regiment

From 1st March 1918.
To 31st March 1918

Confidential

Army Form C. 2118.

WAR DIARY or INTELLIGENCE SUMMARY

(Erase heading not required.)

5th Batt. North Staffs Regt.

Page 10.   March 1918

Place	Date	Hour	Summary of Events and Information	Remarks and references to Appendices
NOREUIL Sector.	1st		Brigade Reserve. Battalion employed on working parties & fatigues	5/5 S.N.H. 57.C.N.W.2. 1/10000
"	2nd		" " " " "	Ow.
"	3rd		" " " " "	Aw.
"	4th		" " " " "	Aw.
"	5th		" " " " "	Aw.
"	6th		Orders are received that the Battn. will relieve the 2/6 St. Staffs Regt. in the Brigade left Sub. Sector on the night of the 6/7th March, 1918	Aw.
"			At 5.25am the 5th Batt. North Staffs Regt. carried out a raid on the enemy trenches in PUDSEY SUPPORT trench between V.20.d.45.90. & V.27.b.10.55 inflicting heavy casualties on the enemy & capturing four of the enemy's one Machine Gun. Our total casualties during this raid were 1 man killed. 1 wounded. Commencing at dusk the Battalion relieved the 2/6 South Staffs in the Brigade left Sub. Section, the relief being completed about 11pm	Aw.
"	7th		The Battalion holding the line as the Brigade left Sub. Sector. The disposition of the Batt is as follows. C. Coy. right front Coy. from U.29.c.92.73. to U.29.c.5.9. took Coy H.Q at U.29.c.31.37. B. Coy left front Coy from U.29.c.5.9. to U.29.c.22.93. Coy. H.Q. U.28.d.48.48. "A" Coy support Coy in RAILWAY RESERVE Coy. H.Q at C.4.b.80.60. "D" Coy Reserve Coy in RAILWAY RESERVE Coy H.Q C.4.b.80.60. Batt H.Q C.4.b.92.56. & R.A.P. C.5.a.75.05.	Aw.

WAR DIARY or INTELLIGENCE SUMMARY

Army Form 2118.

Page 71 Volume No. 2

5th Batt North Staffs Regt

March 1918.

Place	Date	Hour	Summary of Events and Information	Remarks and references to Appendices
NOREUIL Sector.	8th		The Battalion holding the line on the "Brigade Left" sub-sector.	(A)515 SWtds/57.C.NW2) 100 Jin
" "	9.		" "	Jin
" "	10.		Commencing at dusk the 176th Inf Bde were relieved by the 178th Inf Bde, the 5th Batt North Staffs being relieved by the 2/6th Sherwood Foresters. On completion of relief the Batt. moved to MORY NORTH CAMP. The relief being reported complete at 11.30 p.m.	A.
MORY (Nth CAMP)	11		In Divisional Reserve. Company & Individual training & parades for Luthern Company.	A.
" "	12.		" The Battalion employed on working parties. Orders to move forwarded within an hours notice.	A.
" "	13.		" Inspections & Parades for Luthern Ceremony.	A.
" "	14.		" Bathing parade	A.
" "	15.		" The Battalion employed on working parties.	A.
" "	16.		" Parades for Luthern Ceremony. The Batt. received the following changes for gallant services. The undermentioned NCOs & men rendered during the recent raid on the enemy trenches. Cpl R.S. Smith "O" Coy } Military Medal Hqr M Spencer "A" " Pte E Woolley " Cpl M. Paton " L/Cpl J Davis " Pte 2/LS. Procter TMB "	A.

2449 Wt. W14957/M90 750,000 1/16 J.B.C. & A. Forms/C.2118/12.

Army Form 2118.

WAR DIARY or INTELLIGENCE SUMMARY

(Erase heading not required.)

Instructions regarding War Diaries and Intelligence Summaries are contained in F.S. Regs., Part II. and the Staff Manual respectively. Title Pages will be prepared in manuscript.

Page 72. Volume No 2

Month: March 1918

Unit: 5th Batt. North Staffs Regt.

Place	Date	Hour	Summary of Events and Information	Remarks and references to Appendices
MORY (Nth Camp)	17.		In Divisional Reserve. Church Parade.	S.H. S.W. + S.W.1/10000 N.W.2/10000
"	18.		Working parties. The following awards have been received for the Batt:—	
			Capt. J.E. Wenger M.C. awarded a second Bar.	Cas.
			Lt. L.G. Grist awarded M.C.	
			2/Lt. G.E. Yourdust [?] Coy " M.M.	
	19.		Bathing Parades. Commencing at dusk the 175th Inf Bde is moved forward to the position of relieving the 174th Inf Bde in the BULLECOURT Sector. The 5th N.S. [illegible] Staffs	5.25. S.W.1/ Bullecourt Cas.
BULLECOURT (Sector)	20.		The Battalion holding the H.Br. Lancaster Regt on the left Bde Front in the Battle Sector. Relief was completed at U.22.c.15.20. Coy H.Q at U.29.b.35.20. Coy H.Q at U.29.d.05.55. 'C' Coy left front from U.22.c.15.50 to U.21.b.20. Coy H.Q. at U.21.b.30. 'B' Coy in support on TIGER TRENCH & STATION REDOUBT. Coy H.Q. - U.26.b.7.3. 'C' Coy in Reserve in STATION REDOUBT. Batt. H.Q. at U.26.b.7.3. Batt. H.Q (Gns) & R.A.P at U.24.d.30.50.	Cas.
"	21.		The Batt. holding the line in the Batt. left sub-sector. After a heavy bombardment the enemy attacked about 9 am which resulted in the loss of 622 Officers & 55g. The Ranks including the Batt. Headquarters & Staff. During the afternoon the remainder of the Batt. was moved by route march to	

WAR DIARY or **INTELLIGENCE SUMMARY**

Army Form 2118.

(Erase heading not required.)

5th Batt North Staffs Regt

March 1918

Place	Date	Hour	Summary of Events and Information	Remarks and references to Appendices
DOUCHY-LES-AYETTE	21st	(Cont)	COURCELLES-LE-COMTE. About 11/pm the Batt. too arrived at DOUCHY-LES-AYETTE.	LENS 1/100,000
"	22		In reserve. No Parades	
"	23		The Battalion is moved by route march to BOUZINCOURT	
BOUZINCOURT	24		No Parades. Resting	
"	25		The Battalion is moved by route march to BEAUCOURT via MARLY arriving about 8 a.m. Draft of 16 O.Ranks from leave reported	
BEAUCOURT	26		The Battalion is moved by route march to CANDAS.	
CANDAS	27		Bathing Parade	
"	28		At 12 noon the Battalion entrained at CANDAS Station & proceeded to VERQUIN where it entrained to CAUCOURT	
CAUCOURT	29		Parades for Interior Economy & General cleaning up	
"	30		The Battalion is inspected by His Majesty the King.	
"	31		Major J.H.S. Swanton arrives to take command of the Battalion	

T.H.J. Swanton
Major
Commanding 5th North Stafford Regt

176th Brigade.
59th Division.

1/5th BATTALION

NORTH STAFFORDSHIRE REGIMENT

APRIL 1918.

Army Form C. 2118.

WAR DIARY
or
INTELLIGENCE SUMMARY.
(Erase heading not required.)

Place	Date	Hour	Summary of Events and Information	Remarks and references to Appendices

Original

War Diary

of

5th Bn North Stafford Regiment

from 1st April 1918
to 30th April 1918

Army Form C. 2118.

WAR DIARY
or
INTELLIGENCE SUMMARY

(Erase heading not required.)

5th Batt. North Staffs Regt.

April 1918

Place	Date	Hour	Summary of Events and Information	Remarks and references to Appendices
CAUCOURT	1.		The Battalion is moved by Route March to HOUDAIN where it entrained for PROVEN & moved by Route March to the WATOU Area. K.15.d.5.6.	LENS II HAZEBROUCK 5A 1/100000
WATOU Area	2.		Company Training. Parades for Interior Economy. Reorganization of Battalion. Strength Increase 336 other ranks.	A.N.
" "	3.		The Battalion is inspected by the Army Commander.	A.N.
" "	4.		Strength Increase 1 off. Other Ranks. Honours & Awards 2/Lt. H. J. B. Watson & 2/Lt. B. Hayward The Military Cross Individual Training + Reorganization of Battalion. Strength Increase. Capt. + Adj. G. S. Ince. 51 Other Ranks.	A.N.
" "	5.		Company Platoon training. Musketry + Individual training. Strength Increase 2 1 Other Ranks.	A.N.
" "	6.		Company & Individual training. Musketry Strength Increase Lt. W. S. Jaynes. 4 Other Ranks.	A.N.
" "	7.		Church Parades. Company Individual training. 2 Lt. Y. D. Clements posted to B. Coy. 2 Lt. Walton C Coy. 2 Lt. J. G. Dawes. Other Ranks 86.	A.N.
" "	8.		Company + Individual training. Strength Increase 2 off J. L. Lowe posted to A Coy. 2 off W. R. Ollis " A Coy 2 off L. McKnight " B Coy 2 off W. S. Angus " C Coy 2 off P. Shelley " D Coy 2 off W. E. Johns " D Coy	W.S.G.

2449 Wt. W14957/M90 750,000 1/16 J.B.C. & A. Forms/C.2118/12.

WAR DIARY or INTELLIGENCE SUMMARY

Army Form C. 2118.

Volume No 2 5th Batt. North Staffs Regt.
April 1918

Place	Date	Hour	Summary of Events and Information	Remarks and references to Appendices
Watou area.	9		Company and Individual Training & Reorganization. Batt. Muster Parade in afternoon and Inspection by G.O.C 176th Inf. Bde.	W.E.G.
	10		Cleaning up and preparing for move up the line. Entrained N of Poperinghe to White Camp, Ypres and camped for the night.	W.E.G. Belgium 28W 1/20.000 Zonnebeke 28 1/10.000 W.E.G.
Ypres	11		The Battn. is conveyed by train from Saville Rd. to Slieveen Farm D.19.d.25.15 for the purpose of relieving the 122nd Inf. Bde. in the left sub-section of 59 Div. front.	W.E.G.
Passchendaele	12		The Battalion holding the line in the left sub-sector of the Bde front line ~ The disposition of the Battn. is as follows. Right front "A" Coy with HQ at D12.c.02.75. Left front "B" Coy with HQ. at D.6.d.15.10. "C" Coy 2 Platoons in Close Support "D" Coy and remainder of C Coy in reserve at Great Farm HQ D12.w 15.85 Battn H.Q. D.16 d 50.75. Relieved by the 122nd Inf Bde and marches	W.E.G.
Vlamertinghe	13		by companies to Welttje, when the batn. entrained to Vlamertinghe. Casualties 1 O/R wounded.	W.E.G.
	12		Battn. at Red Rose Camp. Moved by march route to huts at Peninghilst. Strength increase Lieut. A.R Cotton 2/Lt A.J Jenkinson 2/Lt C.E Pyatt Lt A.M Brookabank 2/Lt B Derry Rejoined from Hospital	

Army Form C. 2118.

WAR DIARY
or
INTELLIGENCE SUMMARY.
(Erase heading not required.)

Instructions regarding War Diaries and Intelligence Summaries are contained in F.S. Regs., Part II. and the Staff Manual respectively. Title pages will be prepared in manuscript.

Page 76
Volume No 2
5th Battn North Staffs Regt.
April 1918.

Place	Date	Hour	Summary of Events and Information	Remarks and references to Appendices
Reninghelst	13		In Huts at Reninghelst. 2nd Lt C.C. Ryall admitted to Hospital.	
Locre	13/14		Battn move by march route to Locre and camp in vicinity of Locre Chateau.	WD85
	14		Battn now in afternoon towards Bailleul. Transport remains at Locre and at night move into Bailleul for the purpose of taking over the line and relieving a Battn of the 49th Div. from Station on the left to Steambroek on right. Bttns relieved no operation orders issued	
Bailleul	15		In the line. holding the right sub-sector of the Brigade. Battn HQ in cellar Rue de la Gare. Heavy bombardment of the town - Gas shells used. Bttn withdrew from the town in the evening and took up new line, digging in and linking up with 6" West Riding Regt 49 Div. N.W. of the town. Battn front X 11 c 30 85 to X 12 a 2 2. Two companies hot on right and no 2 on left. Transport lines at Locre.	CT&G France Sheet 27 1/40,000
Bailleul	16		Battn holding above line, improving and making supports. Shire heavily shelled in afternoon. Strength however 2nd Lt A.K. Cross. 2nd Lt A. Sammis. Battn H.Q. Convent. St Jans Capell.	WD85
"	17		Battn holding line. Enemy shelling throughout the day on our new positions. enemy activity in the air.	

Army Form C. 2118.

WAR DIARY
or
INTELLIGENCE SUMMARY.

(Erase heading not required.)

Instructions regarding War Diaries and Intelligence Summaries are contained in F.S. Regs., Part II. and the Staff Manual respectively. Title pages will be prepared in manuscript.

Volume N° 2
April 1918
5th Battn North Staffs Regt.
Page 17

Place	Date	Hour	Summary of Events and Information	Remarks and references to Appendices
Bailleul	17		In the line – Casualties Capt Fox, G.S. Sgt Mason. A.H. } Wounded Sgt Emerson, C. Sgt Berry, D. Sgt A.J. Jenkinson 2nd Lt R. McKnight – missing * Since died of wounds.	W.S.S.
	18		Total Casualties Other Ranks 172. In the line. Enemy bombardment fairly heavy. Relieved at night by a battn of 51st Div. Battn moved off by companies to Berthen and then to Boeschepe where they were billeted for the night.	W.S.S.
Boeschepe	19		Cleaning up and re-organization of Companies	
"	20		Battalion entrained outskirts of Abeele and detrain at St Quentin, Poperinghe thence by march route to Peselhoek "X" Camp billeting for the night	W.S.S.
Godlack	21		Battalion move with Brigade by march route to Training Area at Oost Cappel Hazebrouck via Proven and Rousbrugge Haringhe. Battn H.Q. at Cinq Chemins	S.A.
Oost Cappel	22		Battalion + Company Training. Physical Training, Bayonet fighting, Rifle Exercises Close order Drill and march Discipline	W.S.S.
	23		Bathing Parade at Battn. Rousbrugge. Company Training P.T. & B.J. an Assault Course Rapid Loading and Boat Drill Battalion Muster Parade on Belgian Parade Ground, Oost Cappel	W.S.S.

Army Form C. 2118.

WAR DIARY
or
INTELLIGENCE SUMMARY.
(Erase heading not required.)

Volume No 2
April 1918
5th Batn North Staff Regt.

Place	Date	Hour	Summary of Events and Information	Remarks and references to Appendices
Oost Cappel	23		Special Classes for Lewis Gunners, Signallers, Scouts, Runners. Strength Increase Infty. W Woodward Posted to "A" Coy. Officers " E.C. Hurley Posted to "A" Coy. " A.H. Stacey " " B " Coy. " E.O. Davies " " B " Coy. " A.E. Chambers " " C " Coy. " Capt Pyatt " " D " Coy. 28 Other Ranks. Lecture by G.O.C. Div. — to all Bde 7th Officers at Rousbrugge	W.S.E.
Oost Cappel	24		Company Training and Special Classes for Lewis Gunners Signallers etc. Battalion Parade for drill and Recreational Training on Belgian Parade Ground.	
"	25		Company Training and Recreational Training. Officers NCO's and men tested at Bde Gas Chamber Oost Cappel	W.S.E.
"	26		Battalion Parade on Belgian Parade Ground. Extended order Drill and Artillery Formations. G.O.C. 176 Bde present for Officers C.S.M's Platoon Sgts. Afternoon Brigade Tactical Scheme "Defence of West Yser." Bath in Reserve. Whilst reinforcing Battalion on left front, received verbal orders to return to billets and be prepared to move at half hour notice. Moved off by march route from Cinq Chemins via Rousbrugge and Proven to Euronas in field in the outskirts W of Poperinghe	By Belgium 17 Scale 20/30 W.S.E.

Page 78

Army Form C. 2118.

WAR DIARY
or
INTELLIGENCE SUMMARY.
(Erase heading not required.)

5th Batn. North Staff Regt. April 1918

Place	Date	Hour	Summary of Events and Information	Remarks and references to Appendices
Poperinghe	27		"Standing to" all day. Batn. moved off 5.45 p.m. by march route to Ouderdom via Busseboom. Batn. took over line from 18th North'd Fusiliers — 19th Division. to hold Bde left sub-sector extending from Goodtrust Mill G.30.b.8.4 to Grootsbeck G.35.a.7.7. "C+D" Coys in Bde front line "A+B" in close support. Bn. H.Q. Cottage at G.29.a.7.3. Night passed fairly quiet.	Belgium Sh. 28 1/20,000
Ouderdom	28		The Batn. holding the line as above. Position of Coys altered a little and new trenches dug. Heavy enemy bombardment in the evening. Gas shells detected. Casualties 2 O/R killed 2 O/R wounded.	W.E.S.
"	29		Batn. holding line. Heavy bombardment in morning. Casualties 1 O/R missing 10 O/R wounded	W.E.S.
"	30		Batn. holding line. Quiet morning. Boche Plane brought down 600' in front of "D" Coy line. Enemy bombardment of our positions at 4.45 p.m. and Ouderdom to rear of Batn. H.Q. — Casualties 1 O/R killed 6 O/R wounded.	W.E.S.

T.K.O. Maj. for Lt Col

Army Form C. 2118.

WAR DIARY
or
INTELLIGENCE SUMMARY
(Erase heading not required.)

Nov 16

Confidential

Original
War Diary
of
5th North Staffs Regiment
from 1st May 1915
to 31st May 1915

Army Form C. 2118.

WAR DIARY
or
INTELLIGENCE SUMMARY.
(Erase heading not required.)

Volume No 2.   5th Batn North Staffs Regt.

Instructions regarding War Diaries and Intelligence Summaries are contained in F.S. Regs., Part II. and the Staff Manual respectively. Title pages will be prepared in manuscript.

Month: May

Place	Date	Hour	Summary of Events and Information	Remarks and references to Appendices
Ouderdom	1		Battalion holding the line in Bde left sub sector from 9.30.a.8.4. to 9.35.a.7.7.	Belgium Sheet 28 1/W 1/20,000
"	2		Enemy shelling in evening. Casualties 1 O/R wounded.	
"	3		Batn holding line as above. Casualties 2 O/R killed. 10 O/R wounded	a.s.s
"	4		Batn holding line. Casualties 1 O/R wounded.	
"	5		Batn holding line improving and linking up trenches and digging new reserve line. Casualties 1 O/R wounded.	
"	5		Batn holding line. Heavy enemy shelling in morning. Batn received orders to move at noon and left Ouderdom by companies and marched to Camp at TRAPPISTE FARM. K.17.d.2.2.	Belgium France Sheet 27. 1/40,000
Waton	6		Battalion moved at 2.30pm with Brigade by Route march to Waton then embussed to St MOMELIN area to camp at G.33.c.5.5. Transport and 1 Off x 101 O/R proceeded by Route march.	a.s.s
St MOMELIN AREA.	7		Kit Inspections. Fitting up camp.	
"	8		Company Parades. Making up kit deficiences.	ans
"	9		Company Parades. G.O.C. Division presents honours & awards to officers and men of 176 Brigade. The undermentioned of the battalion were	ans

Army Form C. 2118.

WAR DIARY
or
INTELLIGENCE SUMMARY.
(Erase heading not required.)

Volume No 2
May
5th Bn. North Staffordshire Regt.

Place	Date	Hour	Summary of Events and Information	Remarks and references to Appendices
ST MOMELIN AREA	9(cont)		recipients :— 200260 2/Sgt Spencer H.	Military Medal Huybrouck SA
			202950 L/Cpl Paton W.	" 100,000
			201973 Pte Martin E.S.	"
			235043 2/Cpl Birches F.	Commendation card
			41938 Pte Stephens J.	"
			The 5th Bn. North Staffordshire Regt. was disbanded. Operation Order No. 5. attached. The 11 officers left behind as a Training Staff referred to in para 1. were :— Lt.-Col. T.H.S. Swinton (O.S.), 2nd Lieut. K.R. Ollis. (a/Adjt.) Capts. & Botton, Capt T. Bassett, Capt 949 Clement, Capt. Lane S/176 T.M. Battery (Coy. Commanders) Lt. B.A. Smith (T.O.), 2nd Lt E.L. Lyall (Scout Off) 2nd Lt S.M. Price (L.G.O) 2nd Lt K.S. Evans (Sig. Off.) Lt & A.M. Rowley.	
			Decrease in strength, Capt Lane to Hospital	

WAR DIARY

Army Form C. 2118.

Volume No. 2

INTELLIGENCE SUMMARY.

May. 1st/5th Staffordshire Regt. Batt. Training Cadre

Place	Date	Hour	Summary of Events and Information	Remarks and references to Appendices
St Momelin Area	10		The Batt. Training Staff and Transport moved at 5-15 am by march route to Mametz — Operation Order No 1 of 9-5-18 attached.	Appx 16B France 1/100,000
Mametz	11		The Batt. Training Staff and Transport moved by march route to billets at Nedonchelle — Operation Order No 2 of 10-5-18 attached.	Appx 16B France 1/100,000
Nedonchelle	12		Cleaning up.	Appx
"	13		Strength Increase. Capt. F. E. Wenger M.C. Preparations made for moving to Leo Bresses but move cancelled at noon.	Appx
"	14		The Batt. Training Staff moved by march route to billets at Magnicourt-en-Conte. Lt. B A Smith & transport moved to Fiefs to join remainder of Divisional Transport to proceed to Staples.	France 36B 1/10,000 Appx
Magnicourt	15		The Batt. Training Staff moved by march route to billets at Hautville where they will be responsible for the training of the 1st 4th & 5th	France 57C 1/10,000 Appx
			Garrison Guard Battalions.	
Hautville	16		Cleaning up and improving billets.	Appx
"	17		Inspections. Officers reconnoitred trenches.	Appx

Army Form C. 2118.

WAR DIARY
or
INTELLIGENCE SUMMARY.
(Erase heading not required.)

Volume No. 2
May
5th N. Staffordshire Regt. Batt Training Cadre

Page 83

Place	Date	Hour	Summary of Events and Information	Remarks and references to Appendices
HAUTVILLE	18		Inspections & instruction in anti-gas precautions	France S.T.1 App. 4 & 5
"	19		Preparations for move.	App. 6
"	20		The Batt. Training Staff moved by march route to Magnicourt en Comté. see Operation Order No 5 of 19-5-18 attached	France 36.3 App.
Magnicourt	21		The Batt. Training Staff moved by march route to Lillers at Livossart (N.W. of Dieppe)	Magnicourt S.A.
Livossart	22		Inspections 1st & 5th P.G.G. Bns visited	Seb App.
"	23		Inspections 1st & 5th P.G.G. Bns visited	Seb App.
"	24		The Batt. Training Staff moved by march route to Lillers at MAMETZ	France 33A App.
Mametz	25		Capt. Lane reported from hospital. Lt & Q.M. Roxley temporarily attached to 5th Bn. Prov. Garrison Guards	App.
"	26		Church services. Prov. Gar. Bd Bns renamed as under:— 1st Prov. Gar. Gds Bn to be 17th Gar. Bn. Worcestershire Regt. 5th " " " " " " to be 17th Gar. Bn. R. Sussex Regt.	App.
"	27		Weeks Instructional Class for officers & N.C.Os of 17th Worc. & 17th Sussex commenced at Clarques. General subjects under Capt. Wenger M.C. and Sig. Selling under 2 Lt. Evans.	App.

Army Form C. 2118.

WAR DIARY
or
INTELLIGENCE SUMMARY.

Volume No. 2
May 5th N. Staff. Regt. Batt. Training Cadre

(Erase heading not required.)

Instructions regarding War Diaries and Intelligence Summaries are contained in F.S. Regs, Part II. and the Staff Manual respectively. Title pages will be prepared in manuscript.

Part 84 5th N. Staff. Regt. (Batt. Training Cadre)

Place	Date	Hour	Summary of Events and Information	Remarks and references to Appendices
	28		Classes continued. Strength Decrease.	France 368 to 370
	29		The Batt. Training Staff moved by march route to tents at Cargues. Classes continued	368
				369
Cargues	30		Classes continued	364
"	31		Classes continued	365

1st June 1918.

T.H.V. Vincenton Lt. Col.

Commanding 5th Bn. North Staffordshire Regt.

SECRET.

5th Bn. NORTH STAFFORD REGIMENT
OPERATION ORDER No. 5.

Copy No.....

Ref. Map. HAZEBROUCK 5a. 1/100,000.

In the Field,
May 8th, 1918.

---

1. The 5th Bn. North Stafford Regiment will be disbanded to-morrow, May 9th, 1918, leaving behind a Battalion Training Staff of 11 Officers and 96 Other Ranks, as per Nominal Roll forwarded to Os.C. Companies herewith.

2. The remainder of the Battalion will be despatched to the Base, CALAIS, to-morrow the 9th inst, as per Schedule below:-

Offrs.	O.Rs.	Coy.	Parade at	Brigade Startg Point and Time.	Entraining Station.	Train departs at
4.	180.	A.	2.25 p.m.	LES CINQ RUE, 3.0 p.m.	WATTEN.	5.49 p.m.
2.	142.	B.)				
3.	167.	C.)	3. 5 p.m.	Fork Road,	ST.	6.20 p.m.
3.	152.	D.)		HALTE, 3.30 p.m.	OMER.	

Companies will be at the Entraining Station 50 minutes before departure of train.

Dress:- Field Service Marching Order, with blanket. Steel helmets will be carried on the pack. Water-bottles will be filled before marching off.

The Transport Officer will arrange for the rations for consumption by each party on the 10th inst to be at the respective Entraining Stations 50 minutes before departure of train.

3. Two nominal rolls per Company will be issued later for forwarding to the Base with the party. One of these nominal rolls will shew deficiencies (if any) in kit and equipment, also all Specialists or the employment of the man in this Unit.

4. Acknowledge.

(Sd). W. R. OLLIS. 2/Lieut.
A/Adjt. 5th Bn. North Staffs Regt.

Issued at 11 p.m.

Distribution:-
Copy No. 1. C.O.
2. O.C. "A" Coy.
3. O.C. "B" "
4. O.C. "C" "
5. O.C. "D" "
6. O.C. H.Q.Coy.
7. Q.M.
8. T.O.
9. M.O.
10. R.S.M.
11. War Diary.
12. File.

SECRET.

Copy No...

OPERATION ORDER No. 1,
- by -
LIEUT-COL. T. H. S. SWANTON,
Commanding
5th NORTH STAFFS REGT. BN. TRAINING STAFF.

Ref. Maps HAZEBROUCK 5A, 1/100,000.   9..5..18.
        LENS 11, 1/100,000.

---

1. (a) 59th Division Training Cadre (less artillery) is being transferred from VIII Corps (Second Army) to X Corps (First Army) and will come under orders of X Corps from time of arrival in Training Area.

   (b) The 176th Infantry Brigade Group will move on May 10th to MAMETZ Sub-area by march route, and on May 11th will continue the march to TANGRY Sub-area.

2. The 5th North Staffs Battalion Training Staff will move to-morrow, 10th inst, to MAMETZ, accompanied by the Transport.

3. Parade at 5.15 a.m., ready to march off at 5.30 a.m. The head of the column will pass the starting-point, CANAL BRIDGE ½ inch S.W. of S in ST. MOMELIN at 6.32 a.m.
   Route:- ST. OMER - BLENDECQUES - HEURINGHE - ECQUES - REBECQ - MAMETZ.

   Dress:- Field Service Marching Order, less pack.

   Packs and blankets will be handed in to Q.M. Stores by 4.30 a.m.

4. Intervals of 20 yards between every group of six vehicles and 500 yards between Transport of Units will be maintained on the march.
   Units will halt at 10 minutes to every clock hour.

5. The Battalion Training Staff and Transport will continue the march on the 11th inst to FIEF. Further orders will be issued later.

6. Acknowledge.

                        (sd). W. R. OLLIS.   2/Lieut.
                        A/Adjt. Battalion Training Staff.

Issued at 8.30 p.m.

Distribution:-   Copy No. 1.   C.O.
                          2.   "A" Coy.
                          3.   "B" "
                          4.   "C" "
                          5.   "D" "
                          6.   Q.M. and T.O.
                          7.   War Diary.
                          8.   File.

SECRET.

Operation Order No. 2.
— by —
Lt-Col. T. H. S. Swanton,
Commanding
5th North Staffs Regt. Bn. Training Staff.   10. 5. 18.

Ref. Maps HAZEBROUCK 5A. 1/100000
         LENS. II.   1/100,000.

1. Reference Bn. Operation Order No. 1, para 5, of 9th inst.
   The Battalion Training Staff will move tomorrow to FIEFS by march route, accompanied by the Transport.

2. Battalion will parade at 6.50 a.m., head of column outside Orderly Room facing WEST, and will move off at 7 a.m.
   Head of column will pass the Brigade starting point i.e. where ESTREE-BLANCHE – THERONANNE Rd crosses River LACQUETTE at 9.12 a.m.

3. Route:- ESTREE-BLANCHE; RELY – AUCHY-au-BOIS – WESTREHEM – FIEFS.

4. Dress:- Field Service Marching Order, less packs and steel helmets.

5. Stores, etc:- Packs, blankets, steel helmets, and Officers' valises will be handed in to Q.M. Stores by 5.30 a.m.

6. Intervals of 20 yards between every group of 6 vehicles, and 500 yards between Transport of Units will be maintained on the march.
   Units will halt at 10 minutes to every clock hour.

7. Acknowledge.

Issued at 7 p.m.

W.R. Ollis
2/Lt. & a/Adjt.
5th N.S. Regt. Bn. Tng. Staff.

Routine.
Reveille.   5.0 a.m.
Breakfast.   6.0 a.m.

W.R. Ollis 2/Lt. & a/Adjt.
5th N.S. Regt. Bn. Tng. Staff.

SECRET.

OPERATION ORDER No. 5,
- by -
Lieut-Col. T. H. S. SWANTON,
Commanding CENTRE GROUP.

Ref. Sheet 51c. 1/40,000.
     Sheet 36b. 1/40,000.   May 19th, 1918.

---

1. **INTENTION.**
   The Training Cadre of 5th North Staffs Regt. will move to-morrow, 20th inst, to MAGNICOURT-en-COMTE, by march route, followed by Transport.

2. **STARTING POINT.**
   Fork Road J.34.d.95.95.   Time - 5 a.m.

3. **ROUTE.**
   AVESNES-le-COMTE - MANIN - DENIN - TINQUES - CHELERS.

4. **PARADE.**
   Parade outside Billet No. 10 at 4.40 a.m. March off at 4.50 a.m.

5. **DRESS.**
   Field Service Marching Order, less packs and steel helmets. Water-bottles will be filled before moving off.

6. **BLANKETS**, Packs and Steel helmets will be handed into Q.M. Stores by 4 a.m. - Officers' valises by 4.20 a.m.

7. Intervals of 500 yards between Battalions will be maintained on the march. Units will halt for 10 minutes to every clock hour.

8. Acknowledge.

                                  (Sd). R. W. OLLIS. 2/Lt. & A/Adjt,
                                      Training Cadre, 5th N. S. Regt.

Issued at 4.30 p.m.

ROUTINE.
Reveille......... 3.30 a.m.
Breakfast........ 3.45 a.m.

www.ingramcontent.com/pod-product-compliance
Lightning Source LLC
Chambersburg PA
CBHW081502160426
43193CB00014B/2560